# My Childhood In The Holocaust

by
## Judith Jaegermann

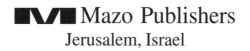 Mazo Publishers
Jerusalem, Israel

# My Childhood In The Holocaust

Text Copyright © 2004 Judith Jaegermann

ISBN: 965-90462-2-7

*Published by:*
## Mazo Publishers
P.O. Box 36084
Jerusalem 91360 Israel

*Website:* www.mazopublishers.com
*Email:* info@mazopublishers.com

Printed In Jerusalem, Israel

# Dedication

This book is dedicated to my parents.

My dearest Mama and Papa
will always be sacred to me.
May God bless their memory.

*Josef Yoel and Rondla Gitta Pinczovsky*

# *Foreword*

For 50 years, the world kept quiet about the geno-
cide of millions of Jews in the Holocaust in Europe
during World War II. There was complete silence about
what happened in the concentration camps and nothing was taught in the schools until the late 1980s.

For Judith Jaegermann, having spent most of her
childhood in the German concentration camps, the
trauma of her experience has been like a bomb inside
her, waiting to explode.

Because she is among the last survivors alive
from the Holocaust, Mrs. Jaegermann regards it as her
duty to tell her story to the young generation of today
so that something like this cannot happen again.

# Table Of Contents

# 1
# *Karlsbad*

I was born on December 24, 1929, in Karlsbad, which is a city in the northern part of Czechoslovakia, bordering on Germany. It was a city inhabited mainly by ethnic Germans for a few centuries and famous for its crystal factories and springs of healing water. People came from all over Europe to treat their ailments.

My parents, who originated in Poland, came after their marriage to Karlsbad. My father worked very hard as a waiter for many years until he saved up enough money and, together with my mother, opened a kosher restaurant. Mother did the cooking and soon this restaurant became famous for its good kosher food and service. It was frequented by the great Rabbis of the time. It had a big golden Star of David over the entrance, with the word "kosher" in its center.

I was the youngest of three girls and had a wonderful childhood. My parents were very religious and kept a real Jewish home. I shall always remember our Friday evening meals, when we sang together and the Jewish festivals, when we were all together. This was the best part of my life.

Being the youngest, I was pampered by my father especially. Until I was six years old, my world consisted of dolls and teddy bears. I loved to play with them. I remember once my sister Esther, 14 years my elder, brought me a doll from Leipzig. I had 28 dolls.

Mama and Papa worked hard, long hours in the restaurant. When Papa came home in the evening he was very tired and his feet ached. When he sat down, I used to bring him a tub of warm water to soak his feet. I would take a small brush with nice-smelling soap and massage his feet. Then I would dry his feet with a soft towel and bring him his house shoes. These were happy moments for both of us.

Once, while he was soaking his feet, I remember him telling Mama about a Jewish family that had come to the restaurant. They left Poland without any money, looking for safety in Karlsbad, so Papa helped them and fed them. Mama and Papa believed in *chessed* and *tzedaka*, kindness and charity, and always told us that this was one of the foundations upon which our family was built. Mama said we even had to help non-Jews.

I was very close to my father. He always guarded over me and protected me from all evil. During a thunderstorm, he would take me on his lap and I would not be afraid of the thunder and lightening.

When I woke up one morning with a toothache, Papa and I walked to the dentist together. He held my hand the whole way and that, too, was such a secure feeling for me – his big hand holding my little hand. After the dentist saw my tooth, he told Papa it would have to come out. I found out that Papa was somewhat squeamish in those days. He nearly fainted when the dentist took out my tooth.

Sometimes Papa had to remind Mama to think about herself, too. Papa made sure Mama went to the very best dressmaker in Karlsbad because he knew that a new dress always made Mama happy. When she came home with her new dress, I asked her to twirl around like a ballerina, so that the dress would fluff out. She loved doing this and we had so much fun.

*(L-R) Esther, Mama, Judith, Ruth*

Mama seemed to always be busy doing something nice for other people on Fridays, as this was one of her ways of preparing for Shabbat.

Almost every Friday, Mama would visit the Rabbi's wife, who was a widow. She took me and my sister Ruth on the visits, but I did not like going. I remember that she wanted us to kiss the widow's hand, but I did not like to do that and could not wait to go home.

Sometimes I did things that were more fun, like the time Mama sent me to the Adler family. The Adler's had a big family, and Mr. Adler was our Hebrew teacher, so when Mama made *challah*, the loaf of special bread for Shabbat, gefillte fish, stew, and cake – everything for a Shabbat meal, she told me to take a basket to the Adlers and tell them "Shabbat Shalom" from Mama. She told me not to make a fuss about it. "Just put it on the table and go play with their children." Mama was a very charitable woman, always thinking about others.

On Shabbat mornings, Mama would take us to the synagogue to listen to the cantor. His voice and melodies inspired Mama so much that when she prayed, she was mesmerized in silence and I could only see her lips move. I do not know where she learned to pray this way, but we would stay throughout the entire service, receiving inspiration from the cantor's voice.

After the services, we would walk home and Papa would recite the blessings for the wine and challah. One Shabbat morning, after we finished eating our meal and it was time for dessert, Mama announced that we were going to have a different kind of treat. She told everyone at the table that on Friday, she had left me alone in the house while she went to do some last minute Shabbat shopping and when she returned, she found out that I had done something that made her very proud of me. I must have been at least six, to have been left by myself.

Here's what happened. A nun knocked on the door and said that she was collecting money for charity. I told her that I did not have any money, but while we were talking, I remembered the special Shabbat cake that Mama had baked, so I asked her if she would like to have it. She said yes, and was very happy, saying that many people would enjoy this special treat. When Mama came home, I told her that I gave her cake to the nun for charity, because I didn't have any money to give. Mama said that now she knew that I understood about being kind to other people.

I remember one time when Papa made the Shabbat lunch. He served us a stew, filled with meat. It was so tasty that Mama said we should really save it to serve the guests in the restaurant. Papa told Mama, "My children are the most important guests I will ever have. Serve them the meat."

Sometimes on Shabbat, it seemed to me that Papa was very nervous and I told Mama I was very concerned that something might be wrong with him. Mama reminded me that because it was Shabbat, Papa could not smoke and that smoking usually helped Papa feel calm, so I should not worry about him.

By the age of seven, I began to realize that we were different from our neighbors. I remember that we had just celebrated the beginning of the Jewish new year, *Rosh Hashana* and *Yom Kippur*, the day of atonement, the holiest day for the Jewish people. My Papa was preparing for *Sukkot*, the Feast of Tabernacles. He was busy making a *sukka* in the yard of our house for us and the guests at our restaurant. I was making the decorations. A sukka is a hut built with green leaves as a roof, where during this holiday all meals are eaten.

Suddenly, stones were thrown from the windows of our neighbors. I was very frightened and asked Papa why they did this to us. He softly said, "Because we are Jews. They don't like us." At the time, I did not know what that meant – "Because we are Jews." I didn't know there was a difference between Jews and non-Jews – since I went to school with all the other children. I didn't ask Papa many questions about what happened because I knew that I would not understand, yet somehow I felt that the world was going to "shake" for the grownups.

Until this time, the closest that I came to knowing we were different was from one incident that I experienced when I was six. There was a Catholic girl in my class who lived in an orphanage. Many times I gave this girl my sandwich because she did not have enough to eat. Once, this girl said to me, "Do you know why they hate you? Because you killed our Lord." I did not know what she was talking about. This was the first time that I heard that someone hated me.

After Sukkot, we celebrated the holiday, *Simchat Torah*, which marked the completion of reading the Torah and beginning again. Papa loved this holiday. He danced with the Torahs so much that he would have to put a handkerchief on the back of his neck to absorb the perspiration. My fondest memory I have of Papa was of him dancing with all the men, lifting the Torah high, entranced in a gaze up to heaven. This was one of the last times that we celebrated the holidays together.

With the holidays over, my sister, Ruth, who was a year older than me, and I returned to school. We were coming home when suddenly one of the non-Jewish boys started beating us on our legs with branches from the trees. My legs were bleeding and I did not know what else he was going to do to us. Somehow we were able to run away from him and get home. Mama took care of me and when I started feeling better, I asked her why they did this to us. She gave me the same answer as my father did. "Because we are Jews." So now I felt a real tremor in my life and I wanted to know, "What is the difference between Jews and non-Jews?"

More things started to happen to us and to other Jews in Karlsbad that indicated times were getting worse.

One day when I came home from school, the Star of David on our house was gone and in its place was a big swastika. I didn't even know what the swastika was. "Mama, what is this ugly thing? Why did they take away our beautiful Star of David?" I started to cry because I knew something terrible was going to happen and I became depressed. I became very quiet and did not speak much after this.

Soon after the swastika was put on our house, Mama said, "We have to move from here, but don't worry. God will help us." These were her words throughout the years, even in the worst times when we were in the concentration camps. These were my mother's words – "God will help us."

Papa never imagined something bad could happen to us. He was a very respected man in Karlsbad, being the head man of all kinds of civic organizations, like the hunting club, the fire brigade, etc. As such, he had many close non-Jewish friends, who called him by his first name. He found it hard to believe that they would want to hurt us. But in the end, when they turned their back to him on the street, he realized that they were not his friends.

# 2
# *Prague*

After the Germans occupied Czechoslovakia, the situation in Karlsbad became worse for Jews and my parents felt that it was no longer safe for us and that we might be better off living in Prague. So they decided to move there. Actually, it was more of an escape. We took the train from Karlsbad in the middle of the night to Prague. We took nothing with us – not even a suitcase. My parents left all of our possessions – clothes, furniture, silver, china – everything. Even my dolls had to stay behind. We never saw them again and do not know what happened to them or who took them.

When we arrived in Prague in 1939, a Jewish committee met us at the train station. They took us to a small flat, which we had to share with three families, kitchen and bathroom as well.

The war broke out. The Germans came to Prague and it was clear that bad times were ahead for the Jewish people. Swastikas were everywhere.

Many things changed for us. The most visible change was that we were forced to wear the yellow Star of David on our chest. This star had to be  strongly fastened to the cloth with needle and thread. It was to belittle us and make us feel ashamed. A curfew was imposed on Jews and we were not allowed to leave our homes after 8 p.m. There was no school for Jewish children. We were only permitted to ride in the last carriage of the streetcar as the front carriages were inscribed with:

### For Dogs And Jews,
### Entrance Not Allowed!

Some of the other signs we saw posted on many of the houses in large letters said:

### Do Not Buy In Jewish Shops

### Jews Are Our Enemies

### Jews Out

### Jews To Palestine

The Nazis would beat up Jewish people in the street for no reason whatsoever. Many times, an elderly Jew could not get up from the beating. He remained on the pavement, beaten up, dead.

One day, the Nazis took my father to jail just because he was Jew. It was very terrible for me. My mother and I went to visit him once a month, but I could not embrace my father. He was only able to poke his finger through the dense grill, and I was overjoyed that I could at least kiss his finger. I loved my father

during which we had to stand very rigidly at attention for four hours at a time. The shouting and the inhuman behavior of the Germans frightened me so much. I remember that it was very hot and I was standing in the terrible heat like everyone else. I could not take it anymore and I fainted. When I came to, a Nazi soldier was poking me in the stomach with his rifle. He said, "There is no pampering here. Learn to stand like everyone else, or you will be killed."

From that time on, during the entire length of our imprisonment, I remained deeply sad and spoke very little. I accepted everything, without making a murmur. This was due to an intense feeling I had, in my deep sadness and despair, that there was just no one to turn to.

# 4
# *Theresienstadt*

From Prague, we were transported by train, in the cattle wagons, to Theresienstadt. I was happy that we were all in the same wagon and I was able to hold the hands of my father, my mother, and my sister. This was the most important thing for me, for all the years, to be able to touch my family. I wasn't afraid of the hunger. I wasn't afraid of the beatings. But I was afraid to be separated from my family. This was my worst fear.

In Theresienstadt, there was terrible confusion. Men, women, and children were immediately separated from each other. My sister Ruth and I were placed in a children's home and we did not know where our parents were.

From the very first day in Theresienstadt, I cried all the time. I was a sad child, because I did not know what happened to my parents. I simply could not get used to being without my parents, and even isolated myself from the other children. After a few days, I decided by myself to go and find Mama. I simply ran away from the children's home looking for Mama. I didn't even tell Ruth, as she was asleep. I was running, crying, looking for my mother. A woman stopped me and asked why I was crying. I said I was looking for my mother, that we just arrived three days ago from Prague. "Where are the Czech women?" I asked, but nobody knew how to help me.

I kept running, crying, asking, "Where are the Czech women?" Then a woman said, look at this address, L315. This is where the Czech women are staying. I could not believe it. I went to the door, and shouted in a loud voice, "Mama." And she heard me. She could not believe her eyes and ears, that it was me, nor could I believe that I found her. Mama wanted to know about Ruth. I told her that she was in the children's house, too. Mama took my hand, after we embraced each other several times from joy that we had found each other. She walked with me to a small room, where she was staying with 12 other women.

My mother asked the women if they would agree to keep me with them. They all agreed and somehow my mother was able to keep me with her. I stayed with her in the same small room together with the other adult women. We slept on the floor. The elderly women made room for me and were happy to have a child among them. They were mostly Czech Jewish women. There were also some Viennese women, and a few German Jews who were so assimilated they knew nothing of Judaism. They felt they were German first of all and did not believe that anything bad would happen to them.

The Ghetto was run by a Jewish Administration for all internal purposes, supervised by the German authorities. We had doctors, clandestine schools, sports, and vegetable gardens.

But when word came out about the inhumane condition in the Ghetto, and the International Red Cross came for an inspection, everything had to be cleaned up, so that it should be a model Ghetto. The world was duped by this show.

And so began our life together with total strangers. Mama was everybody's favorite because she was such an extraordinary woman, so delicate and noble. She was always ready to help and never grumbled. From the time I was able to be together with Mama again, instead of in the children's home, I was able to endure everything better: the bad food, the snoring of the women at night, the primitive washing facilities, and the cold due to the lack of blankets. Although I was generally very depressed, without doubt, I was again the happiest girl, because I could hold my mama's hand. The presence of my dear mother gave me the courage to live for all the years to come.

My happiness lasted only a few days. In Theresienstadt, I contracted a very bad case of scarlet fever and had to be put in quarantine. I saw many children die and thought that this could well become my fate, too. I saw dead children being carried out, their heads covered. When the doctor came, I asked if I was going to die like the other children. "No," he told me. He said the other children did not die from the scarlet fever, but from meningitis, which occurred as a result of the scarlet fever. "You don't have meningitis, so don't be afraid."

When I recovered and was allowed to come out of

quarantine, my mother came for me.

Even though Ruth was only one year older than me, she spent much of her time while we were in Theresienstadt with the other girls. She even worked in a vegetable garden and, together with her girlfriends, was able to make her life as bearable as possible under the circumstances.

Meanwhile, my father was employed as a cook in the Hannover Barracks. Although he had to work hard, I believe that he wasn't hungry. All the young men who got to know him and who worked with him, liked him very much and called him "Pincza", derived from his surname, Pinczovsky.

Seldom did we see my father, but one time we met him on the street. He was poorly dressed and looked very pale. We were happy to be back together again, to touch each other. This was so important. He told us that he constantly worried about us, not knowing our fate.

# 5
# *Auschwitz*

W e had been in Theresienstadt for 16 months when we heard that people were being deported to Auschwitz where, it was rumored, that they gassed and burned people. Naturally no one wanted to believe this. Everyone said that this was impossible and that these were only rumors. Unfortunately Papa, Mama, Ruth, and I were also amongst those to be deported to Auschwitz. They pushed us into cattle wagons, standing of course, no chairs. It was December 1943.

When I heard the lock close on the door, I had a choking feeling, because everything was closed. I could hardly breathe. I shall never forget the bang of this door closing and still have it in my ears. Then my father came to me and said, "Be calm, we are all together." Our fear grew by the hour as we did not know what awaited us. The unknown is something dreadful and is impossible to describe. As long as we were all together, even though we were not living together in the same place, it remained somehow bearable. But what did the future hold for us? Where would we be sent next? Would they separate us? Would we survive? My thoughts were in a turmoil.

We were shoved into the cattle wagons, in the presence of Eichmann, in his flawless uniform with his booted legs spread wide apart. He was observing us unfortunate, unsuspecting people being treated like animals, with that famous crooked smile on his face. Struck with dismay and terror, no one considered refusing or resisting to board the cattle wagons. Everything happened so unbelievably fast, with shouts of, "Come on, come on, you Jewish swine!" while the dogs barked all around. For me, the important thing was that I was together again with my family. The fact that we were together was all important. The continuous fear of the unknown, or that we could be torn apart in an instant, was hell for me and unbearable. We later learned that one can suffer far worse things. A person can be humiliated to such a degree that he/she becomes lower than the lowest animal.

In the cattle wagons we heard nothing but moaning and weeping and whispers that this transport was destined for Auschwitz. Of course, absolutely no one knew anything definite, but everyone had a most terrible and foreboding feeling of what awaited us. Today I cannot recall how long the trip from Theresienstadt to Auschwitz took, but one of my most dreadful memories, which I cannot forget until this day, was that they had placed a bucket in the middle of the cattle car, to serve as a toilet for men, women and children. It was inhuman and demeaning. For the longest time, no one would use the bucket.

As we neared the murderous death machine called

Auschwitz, and the train slowed down, I overheard Papa speak through a tiny opening to a railway employee. Papa asked him if transports went on to other destinations. The employee replied, with a raised thumb, "Yes, up there, through the chimney, which burns 24 hours a day, that's where the transports go." I immediately understood what they wanted to do to us. But how? Would they torture us before we died?

Upon hearing this reply, my poor Papa immediately got stomach cramps and diarrhea. I had to watch how my big, strong Papa, who was for me the most courageous and strongest man in the whole world, had to shamefully drop his trousers and sit down on the bucket in front of all these people. My entire world collapsed around me. I had a fit of shivering and so did Papa. From the moment he got the reply with the raised thumb, he fell into a deep depression. Then Papa announced to us all that we were in Auschwitz.

Many people cried out *Shema Yisrael...*, a prayer that God should help us.

Finally, the train doors were unbolted from the outside and the doors opened. It was night and projectors with strong light were blinding us. We were greeted once again with the barking of dogs and the shouts of, "Out! Out!, Faster! Faster!, Move! Move!" Nobody understood what was happening.

The wagon was very high from the ground. I could not move very fast, I was just a little girl. Someone hit me on my back with a big stick and I fell to the ground. My knees started bleeding. I grabbed my mother's hand and I wanted to ask, "Where are we? Is this hell?" But

beds on the third level opposite me and we had become very friendly as we were of the same age. Suddenly, I heard the two girls reply, "Yes, we are twins." Mengele came closer. They had to come down from the bunks and stand directly in front of him. He looked at them very carefully. Their freckled faces were almost identical. All Mengele said, was, "Come with me. You will be back here again by night." My instincts told me that I would never see my friends again and indeed I never did. He did not bring them back in the evening, nor the next day nor ever. I cannot even inquire about them since I have forgotten their names. I have thought a lot about those two girls. Who knows what experiments this brute carried out on them and how they had to die.

Another time, Mengele came to the barrack. He had been told that a woman was pregnant and wanted to see for himself. He ordered the woman to stand in front of him. When he saw her growing belly, he said he would allow her to live, but his experiment would be on the baby. After the birth, Mengele ordered the new mother's breasts to be wrapped so that she could not feed the baby. He wanted to know how long it would take for the baby to die without eating.

The barbed wire was our only view. We were surrounded by high tension electric wire. Many people committed suicide on the wire. They simply crawled up to the wire and were electrocuted. I can still clearly recall a young girl who did this. One moment I had seen her alive and the next moment she was glued to the wire, dead. She had chosen death by reaching out and clutching the barbed wire. This was hell in its purest form, and it is impossible for anyone to understand without experiencing it.

My mother saw me looking at the dead girl on the wire. She said, "Don't look at her and don't think in this way. As long as I am alive, you will be alive." Then I said, "Look Mommy, she is not suffering anymore. She is not hungry. She is not cold. She is not thirsty and she is not looking for her mother anymore." So my mother took me and said, "Please try to be strong and please try to stay alive."

Likewise, I was very concerned that she should stay alive too, because I knew for sure, without her, I would not make it. So I touched her hand each day to really make sure that she was with me, that I had my mother with me. So many girls had already lost their mothers. My mother was a mother to every girl who did not have a mother anymore.

It was spring when my dear Mama said to me, "Look Laluschka, look at that little bird flying there. I am telling you that this a living sign that with God's help, we will get out of here alive."

I marveled at her optimism because I had lost my ability to believe in miracles anymore and only asked very softly and weakly, "Do you really believe this, Mommy?"

She replied, "Oh yes, I definitely believe that God will help us." This is the answer my poor, starving, yet admirably devout, dear little Mama gave me. How terrible she must have felt to see her children so miserable and hungry.

It was July 5th, on Mama's birthday, when Mengele personally carried out "selections" for life or death. We were standing in line, four rows deep and had, of course, not the faintest idea what was going to happen to us next. Then we saw Mengele direct people with his small stick. The healthier and stronger looking to one side, the elder and weaker to the other side.

With a sadistic smile, he separated mothers from their daughters, sisters from their sisters, friends from their friends. The crying and shouting was unbearable. I still have it in my ears.

We stayed together and rubbed each other's cheeks, so that we looked healthier and more capable of work. While we were standing there, awaiting our destiny, I thought I saw Papa standing at a distance watching the selection process. But I wasn't sure. He was so thin. His clothes did not fit. He looked so miserable. At that very moment, I knew that I had to do something because I felt that I would never see this man again. I tore myself away from my row and ran to him, not listening to the shouts of the women, that they would all be punished or killed because of my leaving the row. It was my father. Imagine, seeing him for the last time on Mama's birthday. I hugged Papa with all my strength and knew instinctively that this was our farewell.

"Something terrible is about to happen. We are either going to be sent to work or to the gas chamber," I told my father.

"Yes I can see that something horrible is going on with you."

I embraced him with all my strength, for the last time. The last thing he said to me was to eat everything that was given to me, no matter what. He made me promise to do this. Then I walked calmly back to my row, looking back at Papa, who stood there weeping. It was fortunate for me that none of the S.S. people had seen me. We continued to stand and wait for what Mengele was to decide for us. I was afraid that Mengele would take my mother. She was exhausted from fear of losing us, too. My mother said, "God will help us. He helped us until now. Don't forget. He will continue to help us." But I personally did not believe this.

Nobody knew at this point, which side, left or right, meant life or death. As if by a miracle, all three of us were pushed to the same side and that is how we remained together. I repeat, we did not know whether this selection meant life or death.

Though nobody knew where we were traveling, everyone said that it could not be anywhere worse than Auschwitz. Today, I can no longer remember how long we rode in those cattle wagons, squeezed together like sardines. We had lost all sense of time. Many girls suffocated and when the cattle wagons were opened, their dead bodies fell out.

We arrived in Hamburg, where we had to engage immediately in clearance work after the aerial bombardments. Hamburg was an industrial city with many factories, so the Americans and British were bombing the city to try to destroy the factories. As I was the youngest and could not keep up with the older girls, they helped me with this hard work. In Hamburg we had more water and were grateful that after such a long time, we could finally wash and drink. Initially we even got a little more food, but then winter came. Again it snowed heavily and we had to shovel the snow from under a bridge in the icy cold. I can remember that during work one day I blacked out and fell into sleep. When Mama saw this, she called to the other women, "Come help me to save my girl, she is freezing to death." Suddenly I felt someone wake me and I saw the faces of many women standing over me. I overheard them saying, "The little one almost froze to death." They let me lie down for a little longer and then several girls started massaging me and rubbing me, so that I started to feel my body, hands and feet again.

I felt miserable, totally depressed and without strength. I got up and continued to shovel snow and wondered how it was possible to go on like this.

Everything was so inhuman, always connected with fear and one had to guard against the S.S. people noticing that one of us women felt ill, so that they would not – God forbid – declare her unfit for work, as there was always the danger of being sent back to Birkenau, which meant death. The Germans constantly threatened us with this fate. This caused us to work above and beyond our strength. Sometimes on our way from the camp to work, in spite of being so hungry, we sang this marching song:

*"This cannot upset a seaman, no fear,*
*no fear, Rosemary.*
*We won't let our life be embittered,*
*no fear, no fear, Rosemary."*

Even the S.S. woman allowed us to sing as this caused us to march faster. And the song itself gave us more courage to live.

Sometimes we saw political prisoners, who enjoyed much better living conditions than ours. They were allowed to receive packages from the outside. On seeing us wretched, hungry, and in rags, they would sometimes throw a cigarette or a piece of bread. Once, an Italian prisoner pointed directly at me and threw a piece of chocolate to me, probably because I was the youngest girl in the group. I wanted the chocolate, but I personally never dared pick up anything as I saw the greatest danger in everything. I knew that anyone found with anything like this would be severely beaten. Before I could even think what to do, another girl had picked up the chocolate and put it straight to her mouth.

When we would return to camp at night, they would search us, even gynecologically, to verify that we had not smuggled anything into the camp from the outside.

Our barrack leader was Trude. She, together with camp commander Spiess, searched us very thoroughly and, God forbid, if they found a piece of potato peel or anything else. The person in question would receive 50 whippings on her naked behind in front of us all, administered with the greatest pleasure by Spiess himself. This saddened me so much, that for days on end, I could not speak a word. Once, a friend of Mama's was beaten like this. She fainted and could not sit for weeks and was all swollen and moaned in pain.

Because of the long period of undernourishment, we all suffered from furunculosis, a skin condition characterized by the presence of boils. I personally had many furuncles, mostly in my arm pits and innumerable ones on my behind. Amongst us, we had a pediatrician, Dr. Goldova, who somehow had gotten hold of a scalpel – probably through the S.S. – which she used to treat us and squeeze out the pus. Of course there was no hygienic care and no disinfectants, so the pus boils multiplied, one disappearing while another appeared. Furunculosis is contagious and very painful. I could not get rid of my boils for months. Once, I developed a high fever as a result and had to be operated on by Dr. Goldova. She was watched by an S.S. supervisor.

However, with superhuman strength, or possibly from the shear fear of being "liquidated," I returned to work. Though I had suffered tremendous pain, I did not want to bother anyone and suffered in silence, until miraculously I did heal. This really was one of the miracles that happened for me. Evidently God helped me to get better, in order that I be able to live out my destiny.

We had many rats in our barrack, which would crawl over us at night, almost as if they were dancing on us. At first, some of the girls did not eat all of their bread right away, wanting to save some for the next day. They put it under their heads when they went to sleep, but the rats came and ate what they tried to hide. So we learned to eat our food immediately, not to save anything for later.

One night, we returned exhausted from work, but the camp was no longer there. It had been bombed by the British and totally wiped out. We had nowhere to put our heads.

Some girls, who for some reason had stayed in the camp that day, had been killed or injured. Our doctor had also been hit and injured. And one of our guards was lying there dead. I can still see the scene before my eyes. And this man was just the only one, who showed us some human feelings and gave us information of the political situation and about the war. We even called him Papi. This is how we came to be moved again – again into uncertainty, without anything tangible, only fear in our souls, hungry and uprooted, not knowing what else was in store for us. The only thought I had, the one important thing, was to stay together with my mother and sister, because that was the one thing that kept us alive. Many women, who were alone, just did not care anymore, they did not want to live anymore and finally died of emotional exhaustion.

So they moved us to another camp in Hamburg and straight away we began working again. It was an icy cold day and even the S.S. woman had permitted us to improvise a small fire, so that we could warm our hands, which were stiff from the cold. Each of us searched for a small piece of wood or paper, which we placed in a pail that we found lying in the ruins of one of the houses, and lit a fire. The S.S. woman had the matches and after repeated efforts we succeeded in getting the wet pieces of paper and a few pieces of wood to burn. Naturally, it made a lot of smoke and smelled badly, but we were happy and proud to have succeeded. The entire group was standing around the pail, their hands stretched out towards the heat. We also moved our feet close to the fire in order not to freeze.

Suddenly, we heard – coming from the ruins – a man shouting, "What are you doing here, you Jewish swine? Get away from here, at once, you scum!" Of course, everybody was frightened, even our S.S. woman did not know who was behind the rubble. Everyone ran away as fast as they could and heard the man come closer. I happened to be the last to flee, as I could no longer move fast. The man got hold of me and tipped the entire contents of the burning pail over my head and neck. I fell from the pain and fear. All the other girls were ahead of me, only Mama turned around for me. When she saw me on fire, she carried me away with all her strength, and cried to the others for help. Some of the girls patted my rags with their hands to extinguish the fire. I was severely burned, but I was lucky that I had been wearing a rag around my head, which prevented me from getting deep burns.

That evening, when we came back from work, camp commander Spiess even ordered that I be given a second helping of soup. However, I was so terrified and unhappy after the day's event, that I could not eat it.

This same Spiess had once almost beaten Mama to death with a revolver, because Mama had found a potato peel. She told me that he had wanted to shoot her, but possibly the revolver was not loaded and so he had beaten her head with it like a madman, until foam appeared at his mouth. For many weeks after, Mama could not go to work and her head was terribly swollen.

My grief at not having Mama with me at work was considerable and I had the most terrible and fearful mental images, fearing that I would not find her again. But the camp leader kept her busy in the camp during her illness.

We had become very emaciated since our arrival in Hamburg nine months previously. We had gone through terrible aerial bombardments, during which many of us cried, "Shema Yisrael" and often thought that this was the end for us.

Adjacent to our camp was an industrial area, which was the actual objective of the British air strikes. In the evenings, there was a total blackout in the camp, as

Hamburg had been heavily bombed by the British. There had been very heavy aerial bombardments several times during the day and also at night and therefore we could not go to the latrines, because the darkness was so complete, that one could not see anything at all. This scared me a lot, as I could not find my way around, and did not want to wake Mama, who was so tired due to the heavy physical work. That is why I always tried to restrain myself, until the early morning. This kept me from sleeping as I had difficulty containing myself until the morning. In the morning, when we were finally allowed to go to the latrines, we of course lost half of it on the way.

One evening, again dead tired after a heavy working day, we were standing in line with our tin bowls, in order to receive a little of the warm water, called soup. When it became my turn, I was already so hungry and exhausted from standing there that I simply thought that I could no longer go on. Finally the soup was in my bowl. I turned around in order to eat and stumbled in the dark. My entire soup was spilled and I was left with an empty bowl. I started to cry so hard that I shook all over and went to sleep terribly hungry having had no food all day. I did not dare to approach the camp leader in order to request a little more soup.

The day came when the Allies drew nearer and we were evacuated once more. Squeezed into cattle wagons again, I felt I was being smothered. The bang of the bolt being shut on the wagon remains in my ears to this day. After a few days, I cannot recall how many, the door was opened. Most of us were already half dead when we saw other trains with emaciated people in their striped camp uniforms. These people were completely unknown to us and were being evacuated from other concentration camps. Once out of the wagons, we stood again in rows of four and that is how this "death march" started on foot. Again, we had no idea where we were being herded.

We started out as 500 girls – only 18 survived the death march. In the beginning, it was somehow acceptable, mostly because we were happy to be in the fresh air and not crammed like cattle in the wagons. I remember one woman in front of me. She could not continue. She begged the S.S. to kill her. He said, "You will die when I want you to, not when you want to."

But, as we progressed about 100 meters, she sat down by the road, feet all swollen, not being able to continue anymore. She could not get up. So the S.S. came and put the bullet in her back. She rolled over and did not get up. Many other women just died along the way.

Those who could not go any further were simply shot on the spot. I don't know with what strength we continued to walk. It could have been only with the strength of God. Our feet were so swollen. We just went on like robots.

Farther and farther we went, only with the strength of an iron will. I must emphasize again that if it had not been for my beloved Mama, who was by my side, I am sure I would not have survived this march. She gave me courage. She comforted me in my despair; she, who was in despair herself. She was my guardian angel!

My mother and sister carried me by supporting me under the armpits. We had to be strong. We wanted to live, one for the other. I kept asking Mama if she was strong enough to continue. I was afraid of losing her.

Mama was also a mother to all the other girls who were alone, and she always found a word of comfort for them. All the girls sought to be near her and felt protected by her.

# 8

# Bergen-Belsen

After many days of walking, we arrived at the concentration camp called Bergen-Belsen. Although we had absolutely no notion of where we were, we soon found out.

The very first sight we had of this ghastly camp was a huge mountain of naked, dead people who were actually only skeletons. I had never seen such a terrible and frightening sight, even in Auschwitz. I immediately thought that within a few days, we would end up the same way, stacked like these bodies, as we would not be able to hold out much longer. As we had lost so many women on the march to this new hell, I felt that we, too, were nearing our end. The ones who were still alive could move only very slowly; it was like a slow motion film.

The camp was in total chaos. The Germans had abandoned it as the front drew closer and closer. We could hear artillery fire, but no one could estimate the distance from where it came. Suddenly, we saw Hungarian soldiers, or possibly Ukrainians, who had taken over the sentry boxes. They shot, quite arbitrarily, all around and it appeared that they were happy when they hit someone. They took great pleasure and amusement in killing.

A few days later, I personally witnessed when one of these soldiers shot at two sisters, who could hardly crawl anymore. One of them died on the spot. The wailing of the surviving sister was heart-rending. She could only whine and moan.

There was nobody to ask any questions of or to supervise us. There was absolutely nothing to eat. There was no water whatsoever. We were *Muselmanner*, a slang term used in the concentration camps to describe people near death from starvation.

Emaciated, lifeless, thrown together in filthy barracks, destiny brought me together again with the woman whose bread ration had fallen into the latrine in Birkenau. She died on the floor one morning in my presence. Her daughter sat next to her, indifferent and numb. We had been approximately two weeks in this snake pit, without eating or drinking. People died like flies. They simply collapsed. Death was everywhere, and everywhere death was anticipated.

On the morning of April 15, 1945, the British tanks and soldiers came into our barrack and said, "Kids, you are free!!!" But nobody moved, because nobody had the strength left to be happy. We had become so apathetic. It is impossible to describe the condition we were in.

Then began the typhoid fever epidemic. The British, upon entering the camp with their tanks, had thrown canned food and bread to the people. Those who could still crawl ate some of it and the results were terrible.

These people simply died like flies, not being used to food anymore. Mama, my guardian angel, had immediately warned us in a soft voice, "Children, do not touch this. After being hungry for so many years, your stomach is not able to digest this food. Wait and eat slowly. Eat only tiny portions."

I personally couldn't eat anything. I had contracted typhoid fever and my temperature was very high. Mama and Ruth had typhoid, too. Again, it was a miracle that we survived. All around us people were dying. There was terrible misery and despair everywhere. I was so weak, that I could no longer speak and I could only hear as if sounds were reaching me through a thick veil. Some time later, I really believe it was a miracle, my temperature fell.

The British soldiers moved us into the abandoned S.S. headquarters. It was the only place that was clean. They carried us in their arms as we were unable to walk. They even hand-fed us. They taught us to walk again, just as one would teach a small child. They weighed us. Mama, Ruth, and I each weighed about 20-25 kilos (about 50 pounds.) We gained a little more weight and strength, thanks to the many vitamin pills, bread and milk.

Bergen-Belsen was a ghastly camp, without hope or life. The heaps of emaciated naked corpses, being thrown into mass graves, will always remain vivid in my memory.

# 9
# *Free At Last!?*

O n our way from Bergen-Belsen to Prague, after being liberated, we made several stops and were able to leave the train for a few minutes. One of these stops was in Pilsen, (Plzen) Czechoslovakia. When the people saw us, they asked us from where we came and about the meaning of the tattooed numbers on our arms. We told them that we had spent three and a half years in concentration camps and that we had gone through hell. Whereupon these people asked us, "And why didn't you stay where you were? Who needs you here?"

We returned to the train, emotionally shattered. This was the welcome to freedom that we had so desperately waited for?

It was indeed very sad when we reached Prague. I never stopped thinking of my dear Papa, who was most certainly no longer alive. But I still held out hope for another miracle.

Upon our arrival, we received clothes and food from the American Jewish Joint Distribution Committee. Our hair grew back and thus we began to look and feel like human beings once again.

We were told about a transport for children being arranged to Palestine, so Mama registered me with the Youth Aliya. She felt that at least one of us should take this step to freedom, after not having found Papa. Mama decided that she and Ruth would stay in Prague to continue searching for any clues about Papa.

At 16, I found myself alone on a ship, heading to Palestine. Fortunately, I made good friends with people who also came from the concentration camps. They were mostly single people.

When we arrived in Palestine, the British took us to a detention camp in Athlit.

The event that followed became one of the biggest disappointments for me. I was freed from a concentration camp by British soldiers and now those same British soldiers imprisoned me in the Athlit detention camp. I had believed that I was really free, but the reality was that I was a prisoner once again.

I had to stay in this camp for three months, once again behind barbed wire. Being so young, I could not understand how the troops who had liberated us and brought us back to life again, could detain us once more. I cried day and night and could not accept this.

My eldest sister, Esther, lived in Netanya. She had been living in Palestine for the last seven years, having escaped from Czechoslovakia with a group of Jews making their way to Palestine in 1939. Although she was not allowed to visit me, she was allowed to send parcels of clothes and sweets. Many things she sent I was able to share with my new friends in Athlit.

The day finally came when I was freed and Esther

came for me. She took me to her home, where she lived in one room with her husband and son. I was able to stay with her. With all that happened to me, the worst part was that my sister never asked me about what I went through. I expected her to comfort me, hold me, and let me lay my head on her shoulder, but she did not. She saw the number on my arm, but never asked what it was like in the camps or how we managed to survive in that hell.

I married at the age of 17. I met my future husband at Esther's restaurant in Netanya. Even he did not ask me about what happened in Europe. It was like there was a bomb inside me, ready to explode. I am aware of people whose bomb did explode. They simply could not handle this kind of apathy and committed suicide. Others were institutionalized, thinking that they were still incarcerated in the concentration camp.

In 1949, the day came when my mother and Ruth finally arrived in Israel, legally, to begin their life in the Jewish homeland. Although we reached the conclusion that Papa did not survive, to this day I continue watching every new film or picture about the Holocaust, hoping to discover something about my dear father.

In Israel, no one asked, and no one showed any interest about what happened to us in those horrible years. People had their own troubles. Israel was in the midst of its own war and everyone was occupied with building the new country, trying to find jobs, trying to build new lives. Maybe this was the reason, but slowly I fell into a depression because of this.

In 1951, we moved to Ramat Gan and opened a photoshop in Tel Aviv, where I worked with my husband until a few years ago.

When Eichmann went on trial in Israel in 1961, people suddenly started asking questions. And then after the trial, nobody asked any more questions. Throughout the years, my depression has continued. A psychiatrist once told me to write down everything that happened to me. This helped, but it wasn't enough. As hard as I struggle, the fears that infected my childhood continue to fester. My memories will always be with me.

After my sons grew up and I wrote my memories, I attended a course at Yad Vashem to learn to speak in front of people. Since then, I give lectures in universities, high schools and institutions, telling about my personal experiences. Soon there will not be any survivors left to tell the story. I feel it my duty to tell the younger generation what happened so that something like this cannot happen again.

# Epilogue

In 1985, Judith Jaegermann began taking courses at the Yad Vashem Holocaust Remembrance Authority in Jerusalem to learn how to tell her story to young adults.

She was invited in 1986 by an Israeli high school teacher to explain to her students what happened to the Pinczovsky family in the Holocaust. Since then, Mrs. Jaegermann has delivered hundreds of lectures in schools and institutions, like Yad Vashem, Beth Therezin, army camps and even in a prison.

Mrs. Jaegermann has distributed more than 25,000 copies of a condensed story of her memories to further Holocaust education. Her story has become an important addition to many websites on the internet.

In 1999, Mrs. Jaegermann was invited to give a lecture to high school students in Vienna and now travels twice a year to Germany and Austria. She has lectured at universities and high schools in many cities including Vienna, Graz, Salzburg, Hamburg, Heidelberg, and Augsburg, at her own expense, to tell these students what happened to her family and the Jewish people – those who survived and those who perished – in the Holocaust.

# The Pinczovsky Family

*(L-R) Rondla, Esther, Judith, Josef, Ruth*